FRANCIS POULENC

Album of Six Pieces

for Piano

Contents

CHESTER MUSIC

u Valentine Gross

MOUVEMENTS PERPÉTUELS
1918
I

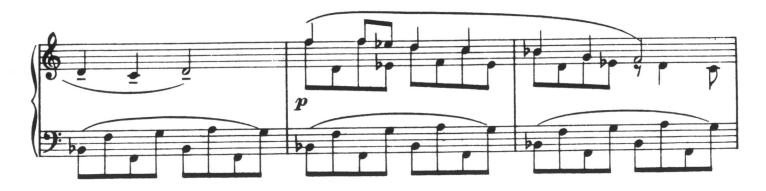

© Copyright for all countries 1919, 1989
Chester Music Limited, 8/9 Frith Street, London W1V 5TZ

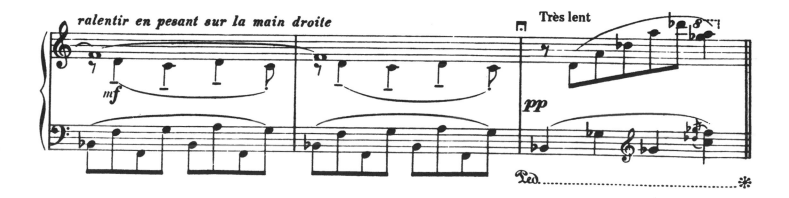

À Ricardo Viñes

SUITE POUR PIANO
1920
I PRESTO

© Copyright for all countries 1926, 1989
Chester Music Limited, 8/9 Frith Street, London W1V 5TZ

6

à Marcelle Meyer

IMPROMPTU No. 3
from
FIVE IMPROMPTUS

à Marcelle Meyer

FIVE IMPROMPTUS
1939
III

Chester Music Limited, 8/9 Frith Street, London W1V 5TZ
Revised edition June 1939

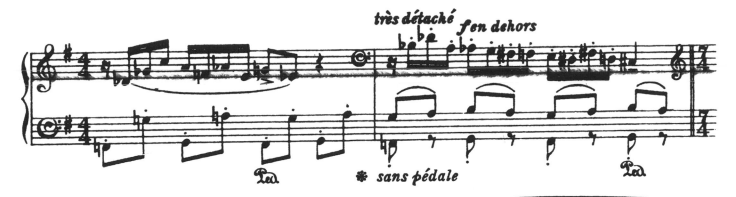

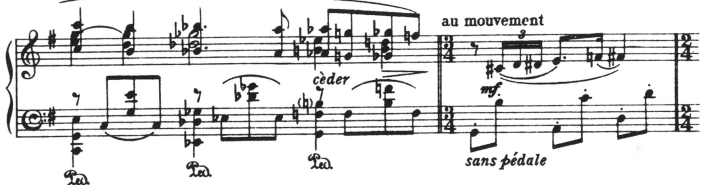

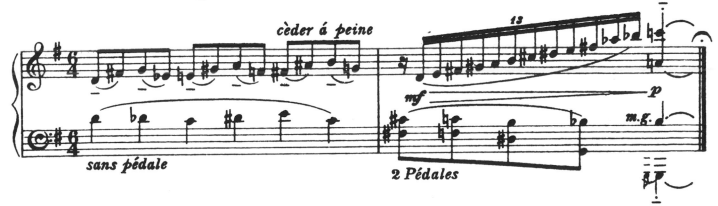

à Luigi Rognoni

FRANCAISE
1939

d'après Claude Gervaise
(16ème siècle)

Modéré

© Copyright for all countries 1940, 1989
Chester Music Limited, 8/9 Frith Street, London W1V 5TZ

Pour ma tante Liénard

NOVELETTES
1927
I IN C MAJOR

Modéré sans lenteur ♪ = 160

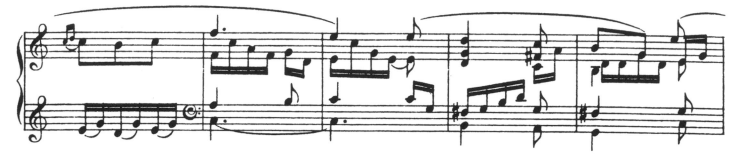

Un peu plus vite

céder un peu

PROMENADES
1921
I A PIED

© Copyright for all countries 1923, 1989

Chester Music Limited, 8/9 Frith Street, London W1V 5TZ
Copyright renewed in U.S.A. 1951

Manuel de Falla

ALLEGRO DE CONCIERTO

(1903)

for Piano Solo

**First publication from the composer's
manuscript, now housed in the Conservatorio
de Música y Declamación, Madrid**

In 1896 when Falla was 20, his parents moved from Cadiz, the city of his birth, to Madrid. He had been making brief visits to the capital for private piano lessons with a teacher of some distinction, José Tragó. The lessons continued, and Falla entered the Madrid Conservatoire, completing the seven-year course in two years. In 1903 the Conservatoire held a competition for a new test piece. Falla's entry was this *Allegro de Concierto*. It won him an "honourable mention", but the first prize went to Granados.

The manuscript of Falla's piece lay forgotten and unpublished among his papers until it was recently re-examined. The *Allegro* represents a side of his activity as composer and performer which he did not want to pursue: virtuoso pianism. With the exception of the much later *Fantasia Baetica* written for Arthur Rubinstein he never returned to this vein (the pianist's role in *Nights in the Gardens of Spain*, although important, is a *concertante* one).

Falla himself gave the first performance of the *Allegro de Concierto* in May 1905 in Madrid, when he took part at Tragó's instigation in another competition, sponsored by a firm of piano manufacturers who offered one of their instruments as a prize. The contest fell uncomfortably close to the submission date for scores for a third competition, for one-act operas, for which Falla entered *La Vida Breve*. This time he won both first prizes.

It was 80 years before the work was to be performed in public again, as part of a recital given by Enrique Pérez de Guzmán in the Wigmore Hall, London on April 24th, 1985.

CHESTER MUSIC

Exclusive distributor: Music Sales Ltd,
Newmarket Road, Bury St Edmunds, Suffolk, IP33 3YB